My First Book About

Food

Felicity Brooks

Illustrated by Rosalinde Bonnet

Designed by Francesca Allen

Contents

2 How vegetables grow

4 Fruits of the world

6 Milk and dairy foods

8 All about eggs

10 Where meat comes from

12 Baking bread and cakes

14 Fresh fish and seafood

16 What is pasta?

17 How we get rice

18 At the market

20 Where do you keep it?

21 Cooking words

22 Making meals

24 Going shopping

Usborne Quicklinks

To visit websites with activities and fun facts about food, go to
www.usborne.com/quicklinks and type in the keywords "first book about food".
We recommend that children are supervised while using the internet.

How vegetables grow

Vegetables grow in or under the soil. Some are the roots, stems, bulbs or flowers of plants.

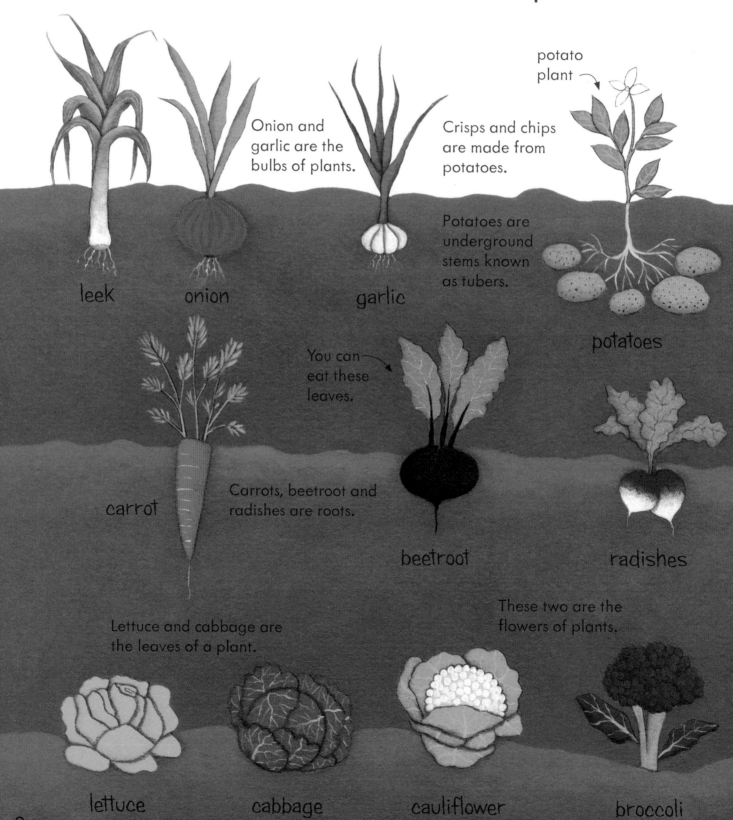

potato plant

Onion and garlic are the bulbs of plants.

Crisps and chips are made from potatoes.

Potatoes are underground stems known as tubers.

leek

onion

garlic

potatoes

You can eat these leaves.

Carrots, beetroot and radishes are roots.

carrot

beetroot

radishes

These two are the flowers of plants.

Lettuce and cabbage are the leaves of a plant.

lettuce

cabbage

cauliflower

broccoli

You can grow most vegetables from
seeds. They need sunshine and
water, and some time to grow.

Add the right
picture stickers
to these names.

turnip

artichoke

squash

sweetcorn

pod

peas

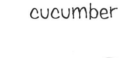

cucumber

celery

pepper

green beans

spinach

asparagus

mushroom

okra

courgette

parsnip

chicory

kale

sweet potato

Brussels sprout

Fruits of the world

Fruit grows on trees, bushes and plants.
Which of these have you tried?

apple

pear

cherries

plum

peach

banana

orange

mango

grapefruit

apricot

lemon

lime

grapes

raspberry

strawberry

Lots of fruit trees
grow together in
an orchard.

pear trees

apple tree

Add the two fruit tree
stickers to this orchard.

4

Jam jar puzzle

Jam is often made from soft fruits such as plums and berries.

Find stickers to put the right label on each jar.

plum jam

cherry jam

strawberry jam

raspberry jam

pineapple

melon

pumpkin

These are fruits, but you can eat them as vegetables.

aubergine

tomato

apple tree

tractor

beehive

plum tree

fruit-picker

Milk and dairy foods

These foods, called dairy products, are made from milk. Add the stickers to these names.

cream   yogurt   butter   cheese

Most milk comes from cows. They go to a milking shed each day so the farmer can milk them.

cow

milking machine   farmer

milk tanker

A truck called a milk tanker takes the milk from the farm to a place called a dairy.

At the dairy the milk is heated to kill germs. Then it is put into bottles or cartons to sell.

A choice of cheese

Many different kinds of cheeses are made from cow's milk. Which would you like to eat?

Blue mould gives this a strong taste.

stilton

This hard skin is called rind.

parmesan

soft and lumpy

cottage cheese

camembert

holes

emmental

Monterey Jack

These cheeses are made from sheep's or goat's milk.

goat's cheese

manchego

ricotta

feta

goat

sheep

All about eggs

Most of the eggs that we eat come from hens. Hens lay their eggs in a henhouse or barn.

cockerel

henhouse

hens

eggs

Chicks are baby hens.

chick

You can eat eggs from ducks and geese, too. Their eggs are bigger than hens' eggs.

duck

goose

basket

Farmers collect the eggs and put them in boxes to sell.

How to break an egg

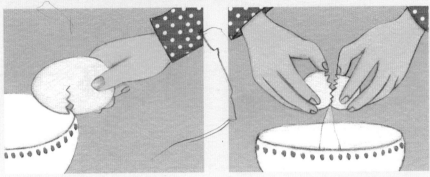

Hold the egg in one hand. Tap it firmly on the rim of a bowl.

Put your thumbs into the crack and pull the shell apart.

Let the clear 'white' and the yellow yolk slide into the bowl.

How do they like their eggs?

These children like eggs cooked in different ways. Can you give them their breakfasts?

Fried egg, please!

Scrambled egg for me.

I like my eggs hard-boiled.

You can buy eggs in special boxes or trays.

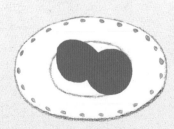

Where meat comes from

Most meat comes from animals that live on farms.

Pork comes from pigs.

pig

Beef comes from cows.

cows

sheep

lamb

Lamb comes from young sheep.

Turkey meat comes from turkeys.

Chicken meat comes from chickens.

Duck meat comes from ducks.

turkey

chicken

duck

A butcher cuts meat up.
Meat has to be cooked
before you can eat it.

pork joint

lamb chops

minced beef

All these things are made from
meat. Can you match the picture
stickers to the words?

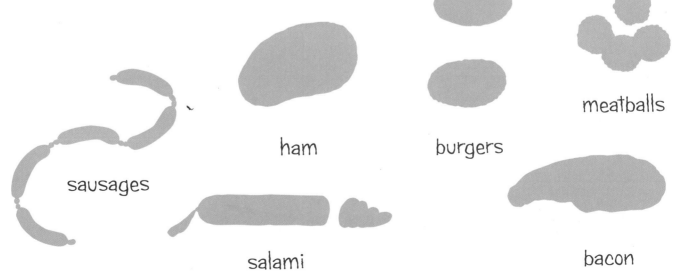

sausages

ham

burgers

meatballs

salami

bacon

Baking bread and cakes

Bread is made mostly of flour. Flour is usually made from a kind of grass called wheat that farmers grow in fields.

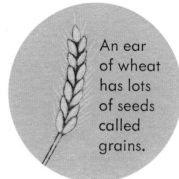

An ear of wheat has lots of seeds called grains.

Yeast makes dough rise.

yeast

Grains of wheat are ground up into a fine powder to make flour.

Bakers mix flour, yeast, water and salt together to make a dough.

oven

kneading

They knead the dough. let it rise, shape it and bake it in an oven.

Different kinds of bread

Have you ever noticed how many different kinds of bread there are? Add the stickers to these names.

Flat breads don't have yeast in them.

rolls

ciabatta

tin loaf

pitta

croissant

baguette

Cake competition

Bakers make cakes from flour, butter, sugar and eggs. Then they add other flavours and toppings. These beautiful cakes are in a baking competition.

Which cake is going to win?

Use the stickers to show which cakes you think should win 1st, 2nd and 3rd prize.

Fresh fish and seafood

Most fish live wild in rivers, lakes and the sea, but some fish that we eat come from fish farms.

fishing boat

Fish live in water and people use nets or fishing rods to catch them.

fisherman

net

All these fish live in the sea.

cod

plaice

haddock

tuna

mackerel

sardine

salmon

There are lots of other things from the sea that you can eat. They are called seafood. Can you match the picture stickers to the words?

prawn   crab   squid   octopus

lobster   oysters   clams   mussels

If you look at a fish counter, you can see different kinds of fish and seafood.

Fran's Fish

red mullet

smoked haddock

salmon

clams

scallops

What is pasta?

Pasta is made from a kind of wheat flour mixed with eggs or water and salt.

To make pasta, you mix eggs with flour and salt to form a dough.

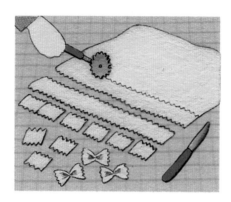

Then you roll the dough out until it is very thin and cut it into shapes.

A pasta machine can help you roll the pasta out thinly and shape it.

You can buy all kinds of pasta shapes to cook. Pasta comes from Italy, so the shapes have Italian names.

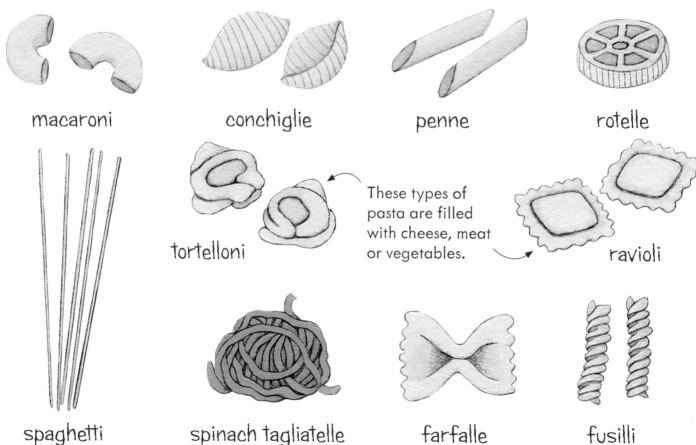

macaroni

conchiglie

penne

rotelle

tortelloni

These types of pasta are filled with cheese, meat or vegetables.

ravioli

spaghetti

spinach tagliatelle

farfalle

fusilli

How we get rice

Rice grows on plants. There are more than 8,000 kinds. Most grow best in shallow water in hot countries.

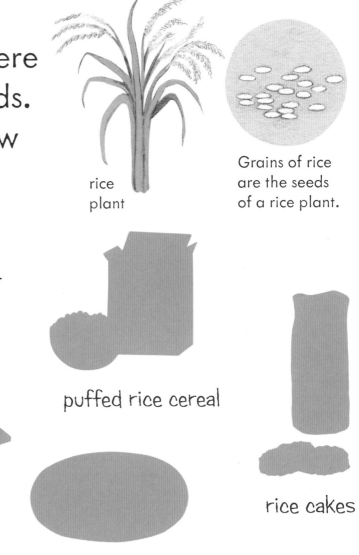

rice plant

Grains of rice are the seeds of a rice plant.

Add stickers to the names to show some of the things that can be made from rice.

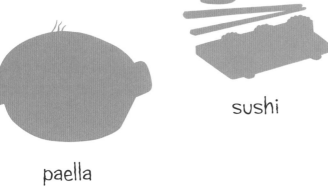

puffed rice cereal

sushi

rice cakes

paella

risotto

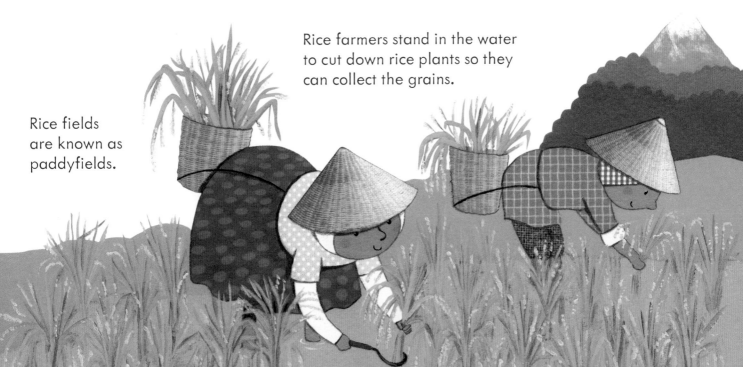

Rice farmers stand in the water to cut down rice plants so they can collect the grains.

Rice fields are known as paddyfields.

At the market

This market sells all the foods you have found out about in this book. Add the right sign to each stall.

Matt's Meat

Frankie's Fruit

Claire's Cakes

Vera's Vegetables

Fran's Fish

Paolo's Pasta

Brenda's Bread

Where do you keep it?

You can buy food in a . . .

tub   tube   carton   bottle

can   packet   box   jar

Cans, jars and packets can go in a cupboard.
Fresh food needs to be kept in the fridge.

Put the food stickers
in the right places.   cupboard

fridge

Cooking words

wash

peel

chop

grate

roll

mix

pour

beat

weigh

fry

pan

pot

rolling pin

scales

spatula

whisk

wooden spoon

knife

chopping board

bowl

grater

colander

Making meals

Use the stickers to make some meals you would like to eat. Don't forget to add some vegetables.

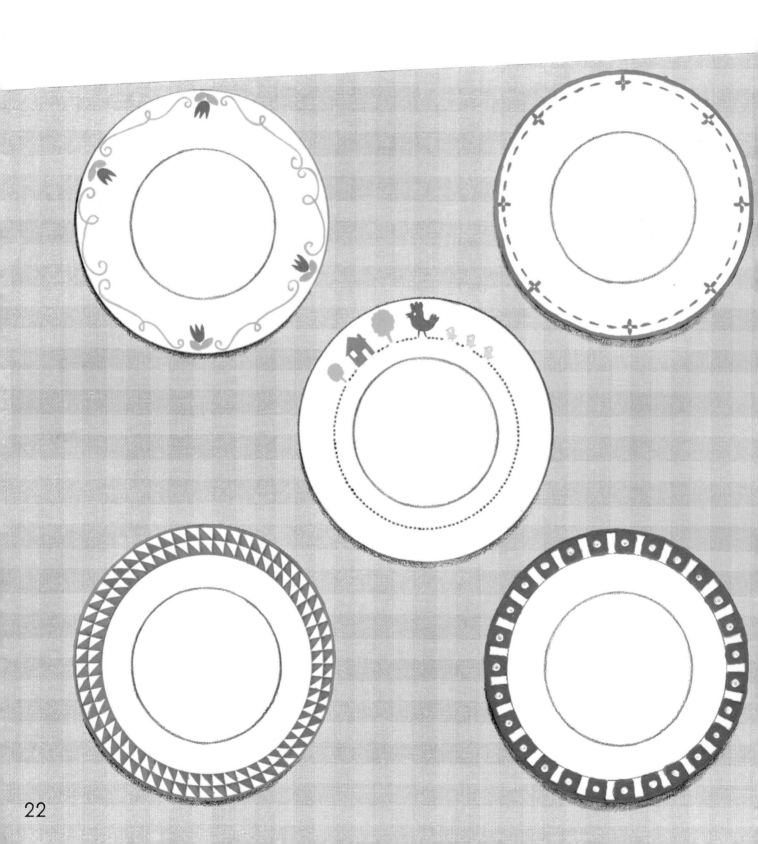

Yum, yum, sausages!

23

Going shopping

When you go to buy food, a shopping list helps you remember all the things you need.

Find stickers for the rest of the things on this list. Stick them on this page. Add ticks to the list if you want.

2 sweet potatoes ✓

1 bottle of juice ✓

1 pumpkin ✓

2 cans of soup ✓

1 piece of cheese ☐

1 pineapple ☐

1 tub of olives ☐

2 cherry buns ☐

2 croissants ☐

3 red apples ☐

3 jars of jam ☐